49 Excuses for Bagging More Candy at Halloween

Copyright © 2019, 2022 by James Warwood

Published by Curious Squirrel Press

All rights reserved

No part of this book may be used, stored or reproduced in any manner whatsoever without written permission from the author or publisher.

Book cover design by: James Warwood
Book interior design by: Mala Letra / Lic. Sara F. Salomon

ISBN: 9781915646279
ebook ISBN: B07YBM9RGV

Book Twelve:
49 Excuses for Bagging More Candy at Halloween

James Warwood

1. THE REAL-LIFE VAMPIRE EXCUSE

I don't want to scare you, but these are my normal eyes and I'm not wearing fake teeth . . .

. . . Yep, that's right. I'm a real-life vampire. This is the one time of year I can walk around the neighbourhood without people screaming and sharpening planks of wood whilst calling their priest. So, give me some extra sweets and next time I'm *feeling thirsty* I'll steer clear of your house.

2. THE FULL MOON EXCUSE

Quick, quick, quick. Give me candy and QUICK! . . .

. . . It's a full moon tonight and the only way to stop me from turning into a werewolf is letting me eat as many sweets as I can. Quickly, I can already feel the wolf hairs sprouting out of every inch of my body and my fingernails growing sharper by the second.

3. THE WITCHES CAULDRON EXCUSE

Do you like my witch costume? . . .

. . . I've tried to be as authentic as possible, with an actual wand and full-size cauldron too. You'll need to give me LOTS of candy to fill this thing. Also, do you have any spare wheels?

4. THE SKELETONS EXCUSE

My name is Barry, and this is Harry and Sally . . .

. . . We are all living, breathing children who need lots of candy. By the way, Barry likes liquorice but the rest of us think it tastes like grandmas three-day old socks.

5. THE GRIM REAPER EXCUSE

Hi, I'm the Grim Reaper . . .

. . . You know, the dude who turns up when someone is about to die, points his bony finger and, WHAM, they're dead. However, I do have a very sweet tooth and I could be persuaded to pass you by if a huge pile of candy were to suddenly appear in front of me.

BOOK TWELVE

Handy, but Spooky Inventions

6. THE HOOVER EXCUSE

Oh, thank goodness. You've still got plenty of sweets left . . .

. . . Now then, it's time to show you my wonderful *Halloween Invention*. If you would be so kind as to open the lid of the sweets and I'll switch on my super spooky suction machine.

7. THE TRAINED HAMSTER EXCUSE

I've been working on my Halloween costume all year...

... I'm dressed as Doctor Frankenstein and this is my pet zombie hamster. Oh no, my hamster has lost control. He has jumped into your house and is chewing all your expensive furniture. I'll look after your candy bowl while you go catch my zombie hamster.

8. THE EGG LAUNCHER 3000 EXCUSE

Isn't she magnificent! I call her the Egg Launcher 3000 . . .

. . . This beautiful little contraption can launch 120 eggs in a minute at speeds of over 60mph and distances of over 100 metres. Alas, I may not be able to even use it. Isn't it a shame that if everyone is generous giving out candy tonight then I will not get to switch it on?

9. THE GHOSTBUSTER EXCUSE

I don't want to alarm you but there is a *ghost* in your house . . .

. . . Fear not, for I am a trained and licensed Ghostbuster. I'll catch the ghost in exchange for all your remaining candy.

10. THE CANDY DETECTOR EXCUSE

You've run out of candy? Are you sure you don't want to change your answer? . . .

. . . My Candy Detector is telling me there is a cake in your fridge, Haribo in the attic and chocolate bars stashed under the floorboards. I can wait here while you get me something, preferably the chocolate, please.

BOOK TWELVE

The Perfect Technique

HALLOWEEN EXCUSES

11. THE STICKY EXCUSE

I am ready to pick out my candy . . .

. . . Before I do so a quick word of warning. I'm going to struggle to adhere to the one candy rule. You see, I have naturally sticky fingers.

12. THE ART OF DISTRACTION EXCUSE

Trick or WOOOOOW WHAT IS THAT BEHIND YOU!!!?!!! . . .

. . . *[While their back is turned grab what you can]* Sorry, I thought I saw a ghost. Well then, best be off now that my candy bag is full. Bye.

13. THE SLEIGHT OF HAND EXCUSE

I understand. You have a strict one candy per child rule . . .

. . . Has anyone ever told you that you have a lovely hallway? *[While they giggle with joy from the fake compliment, take a handful of sweets and hide it up your sleeve].* That's a delightful lampshade. Well then, I'll take my one allotted candy and bid you farewell.

14. THE MOONLIGHT SERENADE EXCUSE

Hello. I'm a zombie who enjoys playing the harp . . .

. . . You look stressed. Sit down, relax and enjoy the soothing sounds of my harp serenading you in the moonlight as you peacefully doze off for a nap. Don't worry, I'll look after the candy while you are asleep.

15. THE HALLOWEEN YOGA EXCUSE

Hello and welcome to Halloween Yoga . . .

. . . Just because it's the spookiest night of the year doesn't mean you have to feel stressed. Join me, your Mummy Yoga Instructor, in the Corpse Position. Lie down and still your body and mind. Breathe in as you ignore the hand rummaging around for candy. Breathe out as I run away with as many sweets as I can carry.

BOOK TWELVE

Turning Halloween into a Business

HALLOWEEN EXCUSES

16. THE FRANCHISING EXCUSE

This year I had an epiphany . . .

. . . Instead of running around collecting candy on my own I should teach other kids my amazing techniques and, in return, receive 10% of their profits. I now have enough sugar to give my whole school diabetes.

17. THE TRADE EXCUSE

I hear adults enjoy eating fruit and vegetables and children enjoy eating sweets and chocolate . . .

. . . Let's make a trade. My bowl of fruit and veg for your bowl of Halloween candy. And I'll throw in this Magikarp Pokemon Card free of charge, which happens to be one of the rarest Pokemon trading cards in the world.

18. THE TRUST-WORTHY KID EXCUSE

Tonight I'm offering a fantastic service...

... Every time you open the door a horrible draft blows up your dressing gown. Give me your candy and I'll evenly distribute them between all the kids in the neighbourhood so you can watch that TV series you've been looking forward to with a nice cup of tea in peace.

19. THE PRICELESS OFFER EXCUSE

Listen carefully, I'm about to offer you something priceless . . .

. . . I, your friendly neighbourhood kid, will give you all the gossip on the street, unlimited access to the play park supervised by me and my gang, and I'll grass up my friend who stole your garden gnome. All you need to do is give me the rest of your candy. This is a once in a lifetime offer, so what will it be?

20. THE C.E.O. EXCUSE

Good evening, it's time for your Audit . . .

C.E.O. of HALLOWEEN

. . . As C.E.O. of Halloween, I have been checking your neighbourhood to ensure the high sweets standards I expect are being met. So please hand over all your remaining candy for inspection.

BOOK TWELVE

Forgot to Dress in a Costume?

HALLOWEEN EXCUSES

21. THE MUGGLE EXCUSE

But I am dressed for Halloween. I'm a *muggle*...

... You know, non-magic folk. There are too many kids dressing up as wizards and witches these days so I thought I'd make sure the muggles get fair representation this year.

22. THE TRAGIC ACCIDENT EXCUSE

I lost my parents in a tragic Halloween-related accident...

... I don't want to talk about it. I'd rather drown my sorrows in sweets and chocolate.

23. THE MATHS TEACHER EXCUSE

For Halloween this year I decided I would dress in the scariest costume I could think of . . .

. . . I'm dressed as a Maths Teacher! I am knocking on people's doors to collect super impossible algebra homework. Scary costume, right!

24. THE VR GOGGLES EXCUSE

What are you talking about, I have made an effort. I'm wearing a *VR Halloween Costume* . . .

. . . What's VR, you ask. It stands for *Virtual Reality* and means you've got to wear these special goggles to see my amazing and realistic computer-generated Frankenstein costume. Now put down that big bag of candy and put on these goggles.

25. THE NIGHTMARE EXCUSE

I know I'm not wearing a costume. Its because I don't want to scare you . . .

. . . Not yet. You see, I'm a living nightmare. So, if you don't give me lots of candy I'll crawl into your head while you're sleeping and haunt your dreams for the rest of your life.

BOOK TWELVE

White Lies (with a tiny smudge of black)

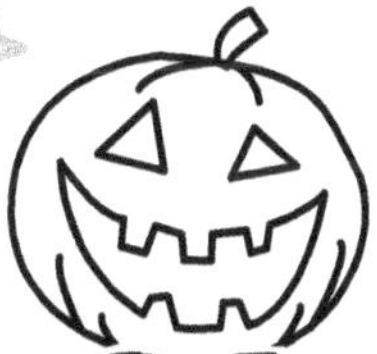

HALLOWEEN EXCUSES

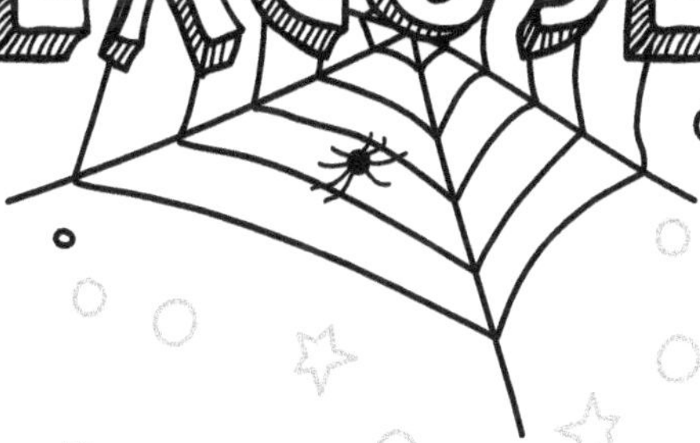

26. THE SICK OLDER SISTER EXCUSE

Please sir, give generously to my sick older sister...

...This might be her last Halloween before she becomes extremely hormonal, starts growing armpit hair and sprouts disgusting spots all over her face. Help make her *last* Halloween special by giving her all your candy!

27. THE BEST COSTUME EXCUSE

Do you like my costume? . . .

. . . Thanks. You do know that you are supposed to give extra candy to the kid with the best costume, right? It's the most ancient and sacred rule of Halloween.

28. THE SUGAR-FREE KIDS EXCUSE

I'm sorry to interrupt but I have some very important information...

... The kids who are behind me are severely diabetic. That means if a gram of sugar touches their tongue they could lose all their fingers and toes and Minecraft experience points. I'll help by taking all your sugary candy and you can take these cardboard flavoured cardboard snacks to give them when they knock on your front door.

29. THE RULE BREAKER EXCUSE

Oh dear oh dear oh dear. Breaking the rules I see . . .

. . . That's a non-regulation door handle, a serious lack of spooky decorations and no sign on your door. I could be persuaded not to tell the Halloween Official Ruling Body if, say, you were to give me all your remaining candy.

30. THE BROOMSTICK EXCUSE

What? I'm a kid from this neighbourhood . . .

. . . I'm Jenny, the Henderson's daughter who lives at number 125. I've been using my motorised broomstick to travel up and down the street because I've broken my leg and not to travel around the whole town collecting candy across all the neighbourhoods. That would be cheating.

BOOK TWELVE

Extremely Silly Suggestions

HALLOWEEN EXCUSES

31. THE QUINTUPLETS EXCUSE

What? No, I have not come knocking on your door five times in five different costumes . . .

. . . I'm an identical quintuplet. Fred is dressed as a mummy, Carl as a vampire, James as a dementor, Logan as an undead lollipop lady and I'm a ghoul with bad dress-sense. Can I have my candy now?

32. THE SPIDERS EXCUSE

Hello, do you know the story of the Pied Piper? . . .

. . . Well, I'm dressed as the Halloween Pipe Piper. When I start playing my spooky tune on this pipe I can either rid your home of spiders or, I can fill your home with spiders. Your choice, which will heavily depend on the quantity of candy you give me.

33. THE YOUR PARENTS EXCUSE

Hi *son/daughter*. That's right, I'm dressed as your strict, overbearing parents...

... Now go get ready for sleep at once, it's well past your bedtime.

34. THE VENDING MACHINE EXCUSE

Do you like my costume? I'm the human Vending Machine from hell...

... I don't accept candy. Instead, you have to insert money and then I'll give the candy to myself.

35. THE UNLUCKY LEPRECHAUN EXCUSE

I just can't take it anymore. What's an Undead Leprechaun without a pot of gold? . . .

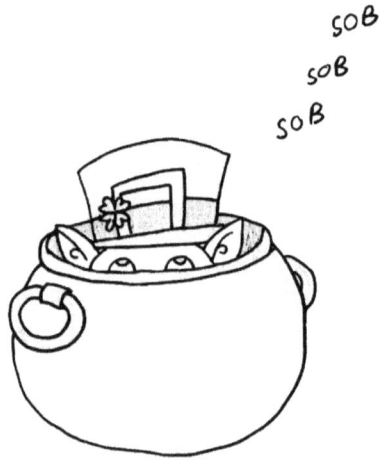

. . . Hang on, do I see chocolate coins? Well, thank my lucky stars. You're a Halloween Angel. Thank you.

BOOK TWELVE

Less Candy, More Money

36. THE DIABETIC EXCUSE

Oh no. You've only got sugary candy . . .

. . . I'm a diabetic werewolf which is a condition that causes high levels of glucose in my blood because of a lack of insulin. Don't feel bad, I'll accept cash, cheque or PayPal payments instead.

37. SPONSORED CANDY FEAST EXCUSE

Hi, will you sponsor me in my Halloween Challenge . . .

. . . I'm raising money for kids who can't afford sweets by doing a sponsored *eat as much candy as you can in one evening* challenge. You can either donate money or sweets, your choice.

38. THE COINS EXCUSE

Only coins, please . . .

. . . No, no. Not chocolate coins. Actual real coins that I can use to buy actual tasty sweets from an actual sweet shop.

39. THE 10P A DAY EXCUSE

Thanks for the free candy but I have a different idea . . .

. . . Just give me 10p per day for the rest of your natural life. (If twenty neighbours agree and give you a 10p every day for 10 years you'll be £7,300 richer).

40. THE CANDY SHOP OWNER EXCUSE

Right then, what you got on offer?

. . .

. . . I've just become a Candy Shop Owner and I'm planning to open my shop in the playground on Monday. I need marshmallows, strawberry laces and foam bananas. Don't worry, I can wait here while you pop to the shops, if needed.

BOOK TWELVE

Too Cute to Say No

HALLOWEEN EXCUSES

41. THE UNDEAD CHOIR EXCUSE

We've decided to spread some Halloween cheer by going from door to door singing carols . . .

. . . Which Halloween Carol would you like us to sing? *Another Noël in the Coffin*, *Love at First Bite* or *Ghouls Just Want to Have Fun?*

42. THE READING EXCUSE

Tonight I have been treating the neighbourhood to a dramatic reading...

... I have the three most terrifying books in my hand. *Macbeth, Frankenstein's Monster or the Minecraft Bible*. You may choose which one I read in exchange for loads and loads of candy.

43. THE FAMILY PET EXCUSE

Have you met our family pet? . . .

. . . Meet Slimy the pet slug. He was dressed as a zombie ninja but he ate his costume. It was my fault for making it out of lettuce. Anyway, if you want you can look after him while I continue trick or treating.

44. THE DRAWING EXCUSE

I made you a Halloween drawing . .

. . . This is you ruling over the whole neighbourhood as everyone knows you're the nicest and most generous neighbour in the world. In fact, tonight would be a wonderful opportunity to prove it by giving out the most candy, don't you think?

45. THE GLOW IN THE DARK EXCUSE

For my costume to work it has to be pitch black outside . . .

. . . You see, I'm a glow in the dark pumpkin. Nobody's going to give me handfuls of candy until they see me in all my glowing splendour.

BOOK TWELVE

Stay Out Later, Get More Candy

HALLOWEEN EXCUSES

46. THE NOCTURNAL EXCUSE

I plan on collecting a record-breaking amount of candy this year . . .

. . . How? By knocking on doors throughout the night until dawn. It fits with my costume, you see, Vampires are nocturnal. I can crawl back into my coffin once the sun comes up.

47. THE MASTER PLAN EXCUSE

Ok, here's the plan . . .

. . . Hit the village at *Happy Hour*, go all the way down Main Street in the *Witching Hour,* come back down the other side in the *Slug Hour* and finish in Section B in the *Tipsy Hour*. Stick to the plan and I'll have the biggest bag of candy in the whole neighbourhood by 10 pm.

48. THE OPTIMUM TIME EXCUSE

I have done intensive research and discovered something amazing . . .

. . . The exact time when your neighbours will be the most generous when giving out candy on Halloween is 8:32 pm. Quick, jump in the car and drive me to the Duke of Westminster's house (the richest man in the world) and we should just make it in time.

49. THE THANK YOU EXCUSE

Hello, I'm the Spider Princess. Trick or treat . . .

. . . *[once you've received the candy, choose one of the following which is most appropriate to each house and neighbour]*

1. Thank you very much *[pause and smile sweetly]*
2. Thank you, I love all of your Halloween decorations, very spooky.
3. Thank you for your generosity and kindness, and happy Halloween. *[It may not work at every door, but those two magic words showing you are a polite young citizen will undoubtedly earn you extra treats].*

BONUS: DEMENTOR'S KISS EXCUSE

Have you ever watched or read Harry Potter? . . .

. . . Then you'll know that a Dementor's Kiss will suck out your soul. So then, pucker up or hand over the candy.

BONUS: HIDING PLACE EXCUSE

Everywhere I've knocked so far has run out of candy! . . .

. . . I put extra effort into making this amazing costume this year *[with lots of concealed storage pockets to hide candy]*. I'm so sad. If only there was some way you could cheer me up. Perhaps something chocolatey with sprinkles on top.

BONUS: CUTE (DEMON) CHILD EXCUSE

Trick or treat. It's the cutest child you've ever seen . . .

. . . (but, if you don't give me lots and lots of candy, I'll put on my other costume and turn into a DEMON CHILD whose head spins around and around with a scream that will burst your ear drums and molten vomit that will melt your face off).

BONUS: WICKED WITCH EXCUSE

This year I'm going to scare the candy straight from your hands . . .

. . . I've been intercepting your mail all year. You had a lot of junk mail, a few letters, and these beauties. They're your bills!!! I think the red one looks particularly scary.

James Warwood is a writer and illustrator who lives on the borders of North Wales with his wife, two sons, and cactus (called Steve the Cactus).

He has a degree in Theology, which at the time seemed like a great idea, until he released he didn't want to become an RE Teacher. Instead, he writes laugh-out-loud middle grade fiction and non-fiction. He also fills them with his silly cartoons. He is the bestselling author of the EXCUSE ENCYCLOPEDIA and the TRUTH OR POOP SERIES.

James likes whiskey, squirrels, reading silly books, playing his bass guitar, and Greggs Sausage Rolls. He does not like losing at board games or having to writing about himself in the third person.

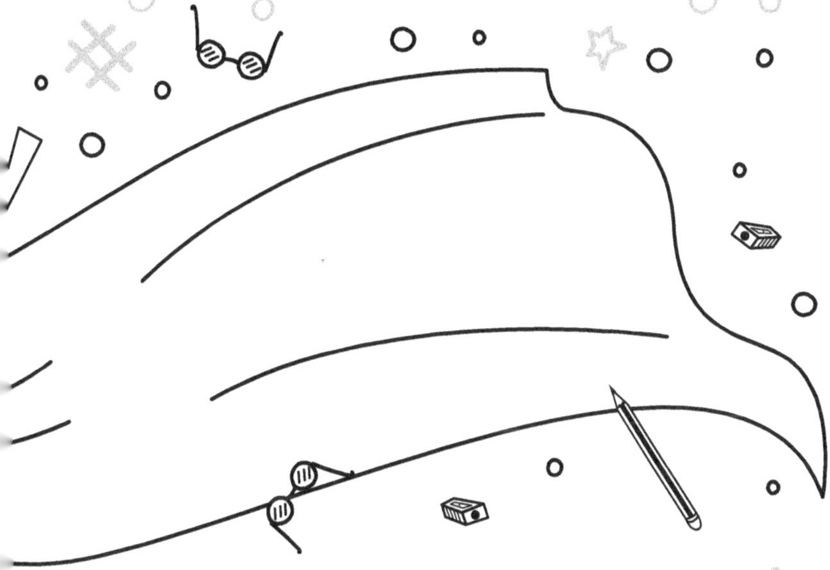

WHERE TO FIND JAMES ONLINE

Website: www.cjwarwood.com
Goodreads: James Warwood
Instagram: CJWarwood
Facebook: James Warwood

Want to join the
BOOKS & BISCUITS
CLUB?

Scan me to sign up
to the newsletter.

MIDDLE-GRADE STAND-ALONE FICTION

The Chef Who Cooked Up a Catastrophe
The Boy Who Stole One Million Socks
The Girl Who Vanquished the Dragon

TRUTH OR POOP SERIES

True or false quiz books.
Learn something new and laugh as you do it!

THE EXCUSE ENCYCLOPEDIA

11 more books to read!

GET THEM ALL IN THIS 12 IN 1 BUMPER EDITION!

820-page compendium of knowledge with 180 BONUS excuses

Scan me to activate your

25% DISCOUNT

www.ingramcontent.com/pod-product-compliance
Lightning Source LLC
Chambersburg PA
CBHW041314110526
44591CB00022B/2907